Headline Series

No. 265   FOREIGN POLICY ASSOCIATION

$4.00

THE U.S.S.R. AFTER BREZHNEV

by Seweryn Bialer

Cover Design: Hersch Wartik; Cover photo: Eastfoto. Kremlin leaders (left to right, Konstantin Chernenko, Nikolai Tikhonov, Leonid Brezhnev, Viktor Grishin and Andrei Kirilenko) review 1982 May Day parade.

The Author

DR. SEWERYN BIALER is Ruggles Professor of Political Science and Director of the Research Institute on International Change at Columbia University. He is also a member of the Executive Committee of Columbia's Harriman Institute for Advanced Study of the Soviet Union. In 1983, Dr. Bialer became the first Sovietologist to receive the most prestigious U.S. award for creative activity, the MacArthur Foundation Fellowship Prize.

Dr. Bialer is the author of many books and articles including: *Stalin and His Generals* (2nd ed., Westview, 1984); *The Domestic Context of Soviet Foreign Policy* (Westview, 1981); and *Stalin's Successors: Leadership, Stability and Change in the Soviet Union* (Cambridge University Press, 1980).

The Foreign Policy Association

The Foreign Policy Association is a private, nonprofit, nonpartisan educational organization. Its purpose is to stimulate wider interest and more effective participation in, and greater understanding of, world affairs among American citizens. Among its activities is the continuous publication, dating from 1935, of the HEADLINE SERIES. The authors are responsible for factual accuracy and for the views expressed. FPA itself takes no position on issues of United States foreign policy.

HEADLINE SERIES (ISSN 0017-8780) is published five times a year, January, March, May, September and November, by the Foreign Policy Association, Inc., 205 Lexington Ave., New York, N.Y. 10016. Chairman, Leonard H. Marks; President, Archie E. Albright; Editor, Nancy L. Hoepli; Associate Editors, Ann R. Monjo and Mary E. Stavrou. Subscription rates, $12.00 for 5 issues; $20.00 for 10 issues; $28.00 for 15 issues. Single copy price $3.00. Discount 25% on 10 to 99 copies; 30% on 100 to 499; 35% on 500 to 999; 40% on 1,000 or more. Payment must accompany order for $6 or less. Second-class postage paid at New York, N.Y. POSTMASTER: Send address changes to HEADLINE SERIES, Foreign Policy Association, 205 Lexington Ave., New York, N.Y. 10016. Copyright 1983 by Foreign Policy Association, Inc. Composed and printed at Science Press, Ephrata, Pa.

Library of Congress Catalog No. 83-83061
ISBN 0-87124-086-6

Introduction

In the second half of the 20th century, Soviet-American relations constitute the central axis of world politics. The two gigantic superpowers compete with each other in the global arena in all dimensions of human endeavor: political, economic, military, ideological, and cultural. But most importantly, their immense nuclear arsenals, their potential to destroy each other many times over, and in the process to destroy human life on earth, make the Soviet-American conflict the central fact of world history, today and for many decades to come. How to regulate this conflict, how to assure cooperation of the two contending powers to prevent war in the interest of all humanity, while at the same time continuing to compete for world influence, are the most difficult and dramatic questions which face us all.

The sources of the Soviet-American conflict are deep and manifold. The governing values, the sense of priorities and the mind-sets of the leadership of the two countries are starkly different. Their roles in the international arena are divergent, the Soviet Union being an ascending, ambitious and anti-status quo power, the United States being a descending, pro-status quo power limited in its international ambitions.

The Soviet Union has only recently reached the rank of a global power, and it is eager to translate its military might and its strategic parity with the United States into global political influence equal to that of the United States. The Soviet Union is pushed in the direction of international expansionism both by the dominant Russian nationalism, which traditionally stressed Russian exceptionality and the messianic role of Russia as the "third Rome" (after the capitals of Roman Catholicism and Eastern Orthodoxy), and by the Communist ideology which assigns to the Soviet Union a historical mission to change the world. Those two dominant currents of nationalism and communism are seldom in conflict in the Soviet Union, but rather reinforce each other.

In the United States' struggle against Soviet ambitions of domination, it is extremely important and necessary to understand the Soviet Union, its internal order, the roots and strategies of its foreign policy, and the direction of its development in the remaining years of the 20th century. The United States and its allies have no choice but to combine competition and struggle against Soviet expansionism with efforts to regulate the conflict to avoid the cataclysmic eventuality of a nuclear clash. Only by knowing the workings of the Soviet political system, the tendencies and zigzags of its development, the mentality of its leaders and leadership groups, and its history can our response to the Soviet challenge be effective.

Even if our understanding of the Soviet Union were not full of misperceptions, there would still be conflict, its sources rooted in divergent interests, values, and ambitions. Yet the conflict between the two superpowers becomes even more virulent, the danger of their nuclear clash more probable, and our attempts to influence Soviet behavior more questionable, when our perceptions of the Soviet Union depart from the truth and are colored by our emotional and cultural prisms, and by our abhorrence of the antidemocratic practices in the Soviet Union.

Today, after the death of President Leonid I. Brezhnev on November 10, 1982, a new chapter has opened in Soviet history with Yuri V. Andropov in the position of top leader. In the Soviet Union this position is of immense importance, with great

Photo by *Time*

Yuri V. Andropov, with Defense Minister Dmitri F. Ustinov, reviews his first May Day parade in 1983 as Soviet president and general secretary.

influence on policymaking—on the substance and form of domestic and foreign policy. At this transition point, it is therefore even more important for us to identify the problems which the new leader faces and to evaluate the likely direction of his domestic and international policies.

When Joseph Stalin died, the Soviet leadership issued a communiqué asking the party members and the general public not to panic. Stalin's death was met in the Soviet Union with grief by some, relief by others, and uncertainty by all. When Brezhnev died there was no need to appeal to the people not to panic, and the grief and relief at the long-awaited change of the guard were, to say the least, muted. Yet the uncertainty surrounding the ascendency of Andropov to the vacant post of general secretary of the Soviet Communist party may be as great as it was 30 years ago when Stalin died. Today, as then, the Soviet Union is confronting domestic and international problems the solution of which defies any but radical steps.

In its 65-year history, the Soviet Union has had only four top leaders: V. I. Lenin (1917–24), the founder of the state, who led the Bolsheviks in gaining and consolidating their power; Stalin (1924–53), the tyrant, whose key role was to use political power to an extreme to shape and transform society according to his own image of what it should be; Nikita S. Khrushchev (1953–64), the innovator, whose primary role was to shock the party out of its Stalinist mold, to institute new policies and reshuffle the inherited structures, to activate Soviet foreign policy and end the Soviet Union's self-imposed absolute isolation; Brezhnev (1964–82), the administrator, who tried to institutionalize the process of policy-making and introduce into the Soviet political system a degree of stability unknown before, and who, in the international arena, presided over the transformation of his country into a truly global power.

The leaders' personality, vision and the power which they wielded were crucial in determining, in their times, the direction of Soviet policies at home and abroad. These leaders played a role in their societies which in other industrialized nations are assumed, to a limited extent only, by great leaders in emergencies. Yet the whole history of the Soviet Union is one of constant emergencies requiring powerful leaders; a history of a highly centralized party-state which has produced powerful figures. The departure of these leaders can therefore be regarded as milestones of Soviet history.

To assess the present transfer of authority to the fifth leader, Yuri Andropov, in its domestic and international context, and its implications for the future, we will discuss the following themes: the Brezhnev legacy and the domestic and international agenda of the successor leadership; the domestic importance of the present succession; the expected impact of the succession on Soviet foreign policy; and the American and other Western policies toward the Soviet Union.

1

Brezhnev's Legacy

Brezhnev occupied the office of the first secretary and then general secretary of the Communist party for 18 years, longer than any Soviet leader but Stalin. While his years in office were less dramatic and convulsive than those of his predecessors, he left his mark on the Soviet system, on the direction of its domestic and foreign development, and on the process of policy-making.

Two points should be made about Brezhnev's role in Soviet history. First, Brezhnev left to his successors solid accomplishments on which they can build, but he also left an even greater number of difficult and fundamental problems which they will have to resolve. Second, Brezhnev occupied his office beyond the point of usefulness to his colleagues, the ruling establishment, and the Soviet people. His major achievements were attained in the first decade of his rule. The last six years were characterized by domestic stagnation, resistance to change and foreign adventures with dubious long-range consequences and clearly negative short-range effects. Brezhnev's rule once again demonstrated the well-known truth that the lack of an established and legitimizing mechanism for transfer of power from one officeholder to another is a costly luxury for a modern state with global ambitions.

The key to understanding the Brezhnev era is to see it not only as an attempt to relieve or arrest domestic tensions and pressures but also as a response to Khrushchev's innovative and iconoclastic rule (just as Khrushchev's was a response to the stultifying and bloody rule of Stalin). Brezhnev's domestic goal was to achieve stability through patience, the avoidance of confrontations among the ruling groups, and steady economic progress for the population. His foreign goal was to translate as fast as possible strategic parity with the United States into global political equality. Brezhnev's era will be remembered as the most predictable and quiescent period in the history of Soviet domestic affairs, and the most ambitious and unpredictable as far as foreign policy is concerned.

Stability at Home

Some of Brezhnev's domestic achievements, although seldom recognized by Western commentators on the Soviet Union, are quite impressive. Brezhnev's greatest achievement was his ability to preserve Soviet stability without resort to mass terror.

Reading the extensive coverage given dissidents in Western newspaper accounts of the Soviet Union, one could get the impression that dissent represented a major threat to the regime. In reality, Soviet dissent had a greater impact on the West; it was more of an international embarrassment to the Soviet leadership than an internal danger. Through tough repression, enforced isolation, and exile, Brezhnev and his colleagues were able to contain the dissidents and even decimate their ranks.

The Soviet leadership under Brezhnev was able to prevent the large educated professional group from becoming a vocal opposition by incorporating it into the Soviet bureaucracy. In the Soviet vocabulary, this class is called intelligentsia, but in reality it has very little in common with the old Russian intelligentsia, an alienated group opposed to the state. The new intelligentsia are members of an upper-middle class that is very much part of the system.

Apart from isolated strikes and unrest, the urban working class in the Brezhnev era was docile. The peasants, crushed by Stalin, began to be integrated into Soviet society and received some of the trappings of citizenship. The *kolkhoz* (collective farm) peasant, for the first time, received an internal passport which made him free to travel inside the Soviet Union and was included in the social security program, which had previously been available only to the urban population.

At a time when colonial rule was long since dead and ethnic groups were asserting their separateness or demanding a share of political power in the West and in the "third world," the Soviet internal empire—the multinational Soviet state—showed remarkable stability. While people in the non-Russian areas clearly identified themselves first as members of an ethnic group and only secondly as Soviet citizens, and while cultural nationalism was vocal and produced tensions between the dominant Russians and the non-Russians, there were very few signs of successful political nationalism or a drive for greater autonomy or separatism among the non-Russians.

The instruments the Brezhnev leadership used to achieve such impressive stability, particularly in the 1965–75 period, were numerous. The first and most important was gross Soviet repression. Under Brezhnev, the Soviet police state with its extensive apparatus regained much of the status and effectiveness which it had lost during Khrushchev's anti-Stalin campaigns. Actual repression, fear of repression, the memories of mass terror, and the all-embracing network of police informers continued to provide the bedrock of Soviet stability.

Another instrument used to foster stability was economic policy. During the first decade of the Brezhnev era, and to some extent even later, there was growth in three areas—investment, military spending, and consumer goods. The latter, notably durable goods such as TVs and appliances, gave a significant boost to the Soviet standard of living, both in the cities and in the countryside, particularly among the new Soviet middle class and industrial workers.

The investment in Soviet agriculture was a very large item in the Soviet state budget. While our perception of Soviet agriculture today as an economic disaster is quite accurate, it should be remembered that the level of production is much higher than it was in Stalin's time. The slump in output in the last four years of Brezhnev's leadership was an exception, the result of four very bad harvests in a row, an unprecedented event in Russian history. The continued import of grain from the West is destined primarily for Soviet livestock in order to increase meat and dairy production.

The Brezhnev era's economic policies were particularly beneficial to the bottom third of the Soviet population. Brezhnev at least partly succeeded in achieving greater equality in the distribution of real income. In the last 15 years, the wages of low-paid workers and peasants increased considerably while the salaries and benefits of the professional classes rose very little.

Soviet consumers, in contrast to their Western counterparts, did not undergo a "revolution" of rising expectations. Their expectations rose, but they remained very modest for an industrial nation. By all accounts, their reference point was the Soviet past rather than their Western or even East European counterparts. Stability was also enhanced by the continuing mobility of the children of Soviet working classes into the professional and upper-middle strata, by their increased participation in local self-government, and, last but not least, by their general apathy toward high-level politics.

The ethnically non-Russian parts of the Soviet Union remained calm as a result of policies which, on the one hand, repressed and purged all expression of political aspirations and imposed administrative control by the Russians, and, on the other hand, permitted a substantial degree of cultural autonomy and private economic activity. The latter provided the non-Russians, particularly in the countryside, a higher standard of living than that enjoyed by the Russians.

After stability, the second most important domestic achievement of the Brezhnev era was in the area of decisionmaking and relations among the leadership groups of various Soviet bureaucracies. There were major changes in the political process at the top echelons, both in comparison with the personal dictatorship of Stalin and with Khrushchev's erratic and confrontational style, which had resulted in a constant turnover of high officeholders. For the first time in Soviet history all major institutional groups in the Soviet Union were represented in the top decisionmaking body, the Politburo. Under Khrushchev, Soviet officials acquired personal security; under Brezhnev they acquired job security. Conflicts among functional and regional bureaucracies were minimal and were resolved by the process of bargaining and compromise. The general secretary's authority was unquestioned but, with the exception of the last few years, it was low key with an emphasis on reconciliation rather than confrontation.

Strategic Parity

The successes of the Brezhnev era in the international arena are indisputable. It was under Brezhnev's leadership that the Soviet Union scored its greatest historical triumph—the attainment of strategic parity with the United States and the Western alliance. *For the first time in Soviet and Russian history the Soviet Union became immune to foreign attack and achieved unquestioned security from invasion from abroad—the uppermost goal of every Soviet leader and one for which countless generations suffered cruelty, denial and terror.* A steadily growing and well-balanced military program enabled the Soviet Union not only to make its own borders secure but also to project forces in the service of its foreign policy far beyond those borders. It became a truly global power.

The failures of the Brezhnev era are even more visible than its achievements. At the 22nd party congress in 1961, Khrushchev declared that by 1980 the Soviet Union would catch up with the United States in the size of its gross national product (GNP), and predicted that this generation of Soviet citizens would be living under full communism. When Brezhnev died, the gap between the Soviet GNP and that of the United States and Western Europe was almost exactly the same as it was at the time of Stalin's death. In 1980 Japan overtook the Soviet Union in industrial production and became the second-largest industrial economy in the world. The technological gap between the West and the Soviet Union, with the exception of military equipment, is probably greater than it was in Khrushchev's time.

At the time of Brezhnev's death the Soviet economy had entered a period of deep noncyclical economic crisis for which there is no remedy in sight. Toward the end of his life, Lenin declared that in the final analysis the historical competition between capitalism and socialism would be decided by which system turned out to be the more productive economically. In this regard the "mature" or "developed" socialism of the Brezhnev era is clearly the loser.

Decline and Death

The stability that was Brezhnev's major achievement was transformed in his late years into a rigid stagnant rule. In making Soviet high officials a gift of security of office, Brezhnev left a whole generation of younger officials frustrated by their elders' lifetime monopoly on positions of power. The Soviet standard of living in the last years of his rule failed to grow or even declined. Soviet consumers still live in a qualitatively different world than their counterparts in the West or even Eastern Europe, a world of drabness, shoddiness and chronic shortages.

The social stability of the Brezhnev era and its real economic accomplishments hid moral decline and decay which permeate the whole social fabric from top to bottom. Soviet culture under Brezhnev remained, with very few exceptions, a wasteland—Victorian, traditionalist and stultified. The lack of innovative spirit and the denial of the right of creative self-expression forced the most-talented Soviet artists and writers into exile. The record with regard to human rights was shameful. While Stalin's criminal practices were no longer perpetrated on a mass scale, they were and still are applied against individuals who dare to disagree with the system or to be different. Long-term imprisonment in labor camps, commitment to psychiatric wards, persecution, loss of jobs, exile and enforced isolation of nonconformists can hardly be reconciled with the Soviet claim to be a civilized society. In this respect Brezhnev's record was probably worse than that of Khrushchev.

In international affairs, the Soviet Union in the Brezhnev era ceased being a model for revolutionary forces in the world, even for countries under Soviet domination. The world Communist movement has for all practical purposes ceased to exist, and, with the partial exception of France, the most influential Communist parties no longer accept Soviet leadership and openly discuss Soviet shortcomings.

Soviet political allies outside of the Soviet bloc have not created any lasting international coalitions, only fragile "marriages of convenience." Soviet economic resources in the service of foreign policy are spread very thin. They are used primarily to shore up the faltering economies of Soviet clients or to provide token help to nations that Russia wants to court. Moreover, those resources are not competitive with the West's. Soviet cultural impact in a world dominated by mass American culture is miniscule. The only significant Soviet foreign policy asset is military assistance and weapons. On the one hand, this makes lasting Soviet achievements abroad unlikely; on the other hand, it escalates the danger of regional conflicts where Soviet interests can best be served by armed struggle or the threat of such struggle.

The deterioration of the Soviet East European empire was symbolized by the unresolved crisis of its most important holding, Poland. It is now becoming clear that the introduction of martial law in Poland was an act of desperation rather than long-range planning. Neither the Soviets nor their Polish counterparts know what to do next. They are in a typical stalemate which carries with it a heavy economic and political price with no hope of early or easy solution. If the stalemate continues, it will pose major strategic problems for the Soviets, since it would create a vacuum in the center of the Warsaw Pact, the Soviet-East European military front facing the North Atlantic Treaty Organization (NATO) countries. Poland is an index of problems faced by the Soviet Union with respect to the rest of Eastern Europe. The monitoring of orthodoxy within these countries no longer seems to provide a viable long-range solution for the continuation of Soviet control. In the Soviet external empire, the process of political, economic and military decline has already started.

In Soviet-Chinese relations, the Brezhnev era saw a dangerous escalation of conflict. Only in the last few years have there been signs of movement toward normalization. Such a normalization will require much more imaginative and courageous leadership than that supplied by Brezhnev.

Probably the greatest foreign policy failure of the Brezhnev leadership was the collapse of the cornerstone of his foreign policy—*détente* with the United States. At the time of Brezhnev's death the Soviet Union had no clear vision of how to restore détente, or how to replace it if restoration proved impossible or too costly.

The record of achievements and failures of the Brezhnev era is clearly mixed. The period of Soviet history over which Brezhnev presided will be known, in our opinion, as a period of Soviet triumphal emergence as a global power in the international arena and as a period when Soviet internal and imperial decline visibly began. *In this sense the Brezhnev era may well be defined as the era of external expansion of an internally declining power.*

From the historical perspective, however, it may well be that the Brezhnev era will be identified primarily as a time of lost opportunities. On the domestic scene the Brezhnev leadership succumbed to its own conservative instincts and to the pressure of vested Soviet interests in abandoning any significant effort to substantially reform the Soviet economy. The first decade of Brezhnev's rule provided the necessary conditions to engage in such a reform: the rate of growth of production was high and the resources necessary for the transition to a reformed economic system were available. Today the new leadership will face the option of reform or decline in a much harsher economic environment, and it will encounter greater social, political and economic barriers to such reforms.

In the international arena the Brezhnev leadership succumbed to easy temptations to exploit the temporary weaknesses of the United States and the Western alliance as the result of the deeply divisive Vietnam war and the Watergate scandal, which led to President Richard M. Nixon's resignation. It sacrificed improved relations with the United States for the short-range, temporary and low-risk gains of adventures in Africa and Afghanistan. At a time—the 1970s—when the military strength of the United States and Western Europe remained basically stable, the Brezhnev leadership sought an illusory goal of "total security," where no level of defense is considered sufficient. Despite détente it pursued unceasingly and at a constant rate the buildup of all components of its military forces. This policy created a predictable reaction in the United States and set back the prospects of accommodation and regulated competition with its chief rival, possibly for a very long time.

Brezhnev's Political Legacy

At the close of the Brezhnev era, the Soviet political system resembles very much a highly repressive authoritarian state, where the force of repression and the enormous police machine are used in a more or less traditional and rational way. Terror is no longer employed to shape behavior and resolve disputes. The state's actions are quite predictable to the citizenry: they are orderly and directed against those who violate the established rules of behavior, and, in their punitive force, commensurate with the weight of the offense.

The Brezhnev era saw the development and spread of a new phenomenon in Soviet society, cultural and political dissent, but the leadership was able to contain it, isolate it, and nullify its influence.

The Brezhnev period was also a highly conservative period in Soviet history. The high officials displayed an overwhelming desire for stability and security. The professional classes directed their aspirations toward material achievements and professional attainments. The population-at-large remained preoccupied with the business of everyday life. The old themes of law and order, national unity, and intolerance toward those who defy these norms remain the ruling principles of Soviet society.

To a degree unequaled in any other period of Soviet history, the Soviet leadership and key groups in the various bureaucracies remained unchanged throughout the Brezhnev era. One index of this stability can be seen in the low turnover in the membership of the Central Committee (CC) of the party, as the figures below demonstrate:

Survival Rate of Members of the CC at Consecutive Congresses

XX (1956)	XXII (1961)	XXIII (1966)	XXIV (1971)	XXV (1976)
62.4%	49.6%	79.4%	76.5%	83.4%

This stability was partly a spontaneous reaction to the experimentation and turmoil of the Khrushchev period and partly a product of the further bureaucratization of the Soviet political system, with its stress on gradualism and orderliness. The Soviet Union entered the 1980s with the oldest leadership and central and regional groups of officials in its history.

The Soviet high officials during the Brezhnev period became

politicized as never before. The cult of top leader, the centralization of the Communist party and state, and the central planning that supposedly permeates all aspects of Soviet life cannot hide the real interplay and give-and-take of politics. The major factors are bureaucratic structures and their subsections, alliances between various bureaucracies on particular issues, and, finally, territorial interests.

The role of one group, the military, requires special consideration because of widespread misconceptions. Without a doubt, the role of the military *factor* in Soviet policymaking is a crucial one: military security is uppermost in the minds of the Soviet leadership. Sometimes, however, an erroneous conclusion is drawn from the role of the *military factor* in Soviet policy, and an exaggerated role is attributed to the *military sector.* Under Brezhnev, the military broadened its powers, but its subordination to the political leadership remained unquestioned, and its role in influencing nonmilitary matters, quite limited. The military's success in attaining a large share of key resources was not a result of its independent political weight, but rather the result of a symbiosis of the views of the military and the political leadership.

The Brezhnev period also saw a very rapid growth of the professional class, especially technocrats and economists. Experts, both inside and outside of the bureaucracy, increasingly provide advice and technical judgment for the policymakers to act upon. They also have a more visible role in policy implementation. It would be wrong, however, to regard the professional class as being composed of cohesive groups. Their organization is very loose, their corporate identity very weak and fragile, and their views and judgments concerning policy issues very heterogeneous.

However we evaluate the amorphous pressures in Soviet society today (the pressure of popular dissatisfaction, the changing living standards, and the changing political situation of the bureaucracies), Soviet leadership is much more responsive to them now than in the past. In large measure, the responsiveness can be described as an *anticipatory reaction*—not a response to the actual behavior of workers but to the leadership's fear that if their interests are not sufficiently considered, their behavior might become disruptive and dangerous. The lessons of workers' dissatisfaction in the East European countries—especially in Poland—have not been lost on Soviet leaders.

In contrast to their Western counterparts, Brezhnev's political heirs still retain a firm belief in the idea of progress. They are committed as much as before to the goal of growth, particularly economic growth. Their belief in the inherent goodness and worth of technological progress and science remains deeply rooted. This is one of the reasons why, despite widespread political cynicism, they retain a basically optimistic outlook. They still define progress by the standards established by the developed Western societies and by the Soviet desire to "catch up."

At the same time that foreign policy and international relations in general attained under Brezhnev greater importance in the Soviet policymaking process than ever before, the connection between internal politics and external policies also became closer. This is partly a result of the Soviet economy becoming less isolated from the world economy and the deliberate attempt to use foreign technology in place of internal reforms to stimulate Soviet economic growth. It is also a result of the Soviet Union's transformation from a regional and provincial power into a global power with changed appetites and aspirations.

2

Hard Choices
in the 1980s

The Soviet Union faces serious troubles and challenges in the 1980s. Although they are primarily economic in nature, they exert pressure on many aspects of Soviet social and political life. To paraphrase the old Marxist metaphor, after many decades when the political "superstructure" molded the Soviet socioeconomic "base," the time has come for the base to take its revenge on the superstructure. To use Marxist jargon again, the relationship between production and the forces of production is "out of whack" and constitutes a profound obstacle to progress and growth.

The list of serious economic problems is very long, and only the most important ones will be mentioned:

▶The maturation of the Soviet economy has led to a decline in its rate of growth. The projection for the 1980s, on which there is very little disagreement among Western experts and no convincing challenges from Soviet officials or economists, suggests a 2 percent to maximum 3 percent annual rate of growth of GNP.

▶Prices, costs and profits in the Soviet economy are artificial indicators that provide no true measurement of performance and little guidance to the directors of the Soviet economy. Soviet planning is still geared to only one indicator, the size of output. This indicator of success does more harm than good because it ignores the quality of products and the real costs of production.

▶The managerial and incentive system rewards primarily the *quantity* of production. The system is too highly centralized in supervising day-by-day managerial activities and too little centralized in its control over investments.

▶The key source of higher productivity—new technology deriving from domestic and foreign sources—has only a narrow influence on Soviet economic performance. It is not exploited successfully by the Soviets to increase the productivity of the economy as a whole. The technological gap between key branches of American and Soviet industry between 1953, the year when Stalin died, and the late 1970s has remained basically unchanged. In the 1980s it may even grow because of the backwardness of the Soviet electronic industry and research.

▶The era of cheap and abundant raw materials in the Soviet Union has come to an end. To satisfy its own, and its empire's, demands, the Soviet Union has to develop the very expensive natural resources of Siberia and redirect part of its investment resources from other goals.

▶One of the original sins of Soviet forced industrialization has come to haunt Soviet development today. The Soviet leaders neglected almost entirely the development of industrial and agricultural infrastructure, and they continue to put off investments in infrastructure to a future date. The point is that the future is now. (The United States, with a population of 233 million, compared with the Soviet Union, with a population of 270 million, has almost ten times more telephones, about nineteen times more cars, six times more trucks and buses, and almost four times more miles of paved roads.) The lack of railroads, paved roads, trucks, storage facilities, repair shops, spare parts for machinery and cars, and communication facilities creates dangerous bottlenecks in Soviet development. It results in the unbearably high level of loss of finished products. For example, the Soviet

Union is the second-largest producer of fertilizer in the world, but the lack of storage facilities on the county level and on collective or state farms accounts for, by Soviet estimates, a one-third loss. Again, according to Soviet sources, about 20–25 percent of the Soviet harvest is lost because of lack of infrastructure.

▶Due to cyclical changes in population growth and the sorry state of Soviet health facilities, the rate of growth of the Soviet labor force is declining and will decline even more sharply in the 1980s. The drop is so precipitous that instead of the 2 million to 3 million new workers who entered the Soviet labor force annually in the 1970s, by 1985 the number might not be larger than 200,000–300,000.

▶Due to the slow growth of Soviet energy resources and stagnant oil production, which are the main sources of foreign currency, the Soviets will probably be unable to increase their hard-currency earnings from the West to buy high technology and foodstuffs, particularly grain.

▶Finally, the chronic weak spot of the Soviet economy, agriculture, which has failed to keep pace with population growth, may steadily push down the rate of increase of the entire Soviet GNP. (The working population in Soviet agriculture constitutes 20 percent of the total working population.)

The Soviet economy in the 1980s confronts the planners with extremely difficult dilemmas. To increase labor productivity, major sums have to be spent on technology, on the consumer goods that provide incentives for the work force, and on speeding up the development of the infrastructure. Yet the rate of growth of investments—and even their absolute size—will be lower in the 1980s than in the 1970s. Cuts in the growth of military expenditures or even in their overall size would alleviate the situation only slightly. In any event they are not likely to be undertaken in the present international climate. Without economic development on a broad front, for which the present system is not geared, even the high-priority growth of military production will suffer in the 1980s.

The economic difficulties of the Soviet Union may have important consequences for social stability in the 1980s. The chief potential danger to social stability may come from the industrial workers. The urban working classes became used to a steady growth in their standard of living in the 1960s and 1970s. How they will react to years of stagnation or even decline of their living standard is difficult to predict. Any serious industrial reform will require austerity on their part. Subsidies for basic consumer goods and services will have to be cut and work and productivity increased. In this period opportunities to move into the middle and professional classes will continue to diminish due to the competition of a by now quite large Soviet middle class and because Soviet higher education expenditures are stagnating. The combination of these factors may erode the patience and political apathy of the Soviet workers.

During the Khrushchev and Brezhnev eras another potential source of social instability—the non-Russian nations in the U.S.S.R.—was handled on the whole successfully by the Soviet leadership by a policy of "stick" and "carrot." On the one hand, the police control of the non-Russian population centers was very thorough and fast in its reaction to any signs of dissent; on the other hand, the economic policy of Moscow assured the non-Russian population, particularly the rural population, a standard of living higher than in the rest of the country. But the job of preserving the social peace of the multinational Soviet state will become more difficult because the economic base—and along with it the "carrot"—will to some degree erode.

However, the widespread view in the West that the nationalities problem will constitute a key source of social trouble for the regime in the 1980s does not appear well-founded. Although in the *long run* the nationalities problem is potentially the most insoluble and the most damaging of Soviet problems, there is no conclusive evidence that it will become the central focus of social instability in the 1980s. (One should remember that the often-quoted figure showing that the Russians are only half of the population is significant only to the extent that one assumes that the Slavs, Ukrainians and Belorussians, who together with the Russians constitute about three quarters of the population, do not share the Russians' popular or elitist attitudes.)

Social Discipline

In addition to the problems generated by the political system itself, the two most immediate and most important problems facing Andropov are the age-old (common to czarist Russia as well as the Soviet Union) questions of social discipline and bureaucratic inertia.

During the last years of Brezhnev's leadership, social discipline deteriorated to an extent remarkable even by Soviet standards. Absenteeism among workers skyrocketed. The turnover of industrial workers, by some estimates, reached the unheard-of level of over 20 percent a year. The quality of production, let alone services, deteriorated through lack of control and low incentives to a point where it may have actually lowered the level of GNP by about 15–20 percent. The scourge of Soviet society, alcoholism, became uncontrollable. Corruption and thievery became so enormous that, in fact, it amounted to a secondary redistribution of national income.

The visible decline of social discipline has become a political issue because it impinges heavily on the ability of the political directors of the system to achieve their economic goals, and because, in a police state, these forms of deviant social behavior are seen as a mass expression of political disaffection. Without major strengthening of social discipline, no improvement in Soviet economic performance will be possible, and it is economic performance which in the post-Stalin era has become a key source of political legitimacy.

Bureaucratic Inertia

The regime's ability to increase social discipline will require more than coercive measures. The demoralization and the near decomposition of the Soviet working class are so profound and the lack of discipline and disillusionment with the regime's promises are so ingrained that some economists and sociologists wonder if the entire present generation of Soviet workers is not irretrievably lost to efforts to stimulate a greater sense of responsibility and different work habits.

The process of decisionmaking, already cumbersome in the

Soviet Union under any conditions, was made even more intractable by Brezhnev's illness and his necessity to treat his position as general secretary as a part-time job. Bureaucratic routine prevailed in the central and local organizations, and any attempts at reforms were simply tabled. Policy decisions of great importance waited too long to be adopted. For example, the crash program to prevent an energy crisis and increase oil production was not adopted until 1981. Costly policies which, as anybody could see, did not bring results were continued without change: for example, the Brezhnev policy of shoving enormous sums of money at agriculture.

The very low level of horizontal mobility created a shortage of the most important type of party functionary, the generalist, whose skills are critical to the coordination and integration of diverse bureaucracies. "Clientelism"—a system wherein coteries of officials have high-up protectors—became widespread and encouraged large-scale corruption. The most famous cases of corruption and protection involved two of Brezhnev's close friends, the first secretary of the Krasnodar province and the minister of internal affairs of the U.S.S.R. Their corruption was well-known in Moscow, but as long as Brezhnev was alive to protect them they were safe. Very shortly after Brezhnev's death, both officials were arrested.

As long as the old cadres in their late 60s and early 70s monopolize key offices, very little can change in the Soviet Union. The bureaucracy has to be shaken up to provide greater opportunities for officials in their 50s. Until that is done, even a very strong leader in the Kremlin will see his innovative policies sidetracked, sabotaged and absorbed by the system.

Another political challenge that the Soviet leadership is facing in the 1980s is how to preserve an equilibrium among the diverse leadership groups and bureaucracies. The period of great stability of the Brezhnev era coincided with a rising standard of living for *all* levels of Soviet society and *all* levels of officialdom. No bureaucratic hierarchy received everything that it wanted, but every bureaucratic hierarchy received something.

Probably more important than the potential divisiveness

UNION OF SOVIET SOCIALIST REPUBLICS

Current History, Inc.

among the various bureaucracies are indications, gleaned from frequent meetings, discussions and private conversations with officials over a long period of time, that the "spark" has gone out of their thinking and hopes. This is not to say they lack devotion to the regime and to the system, but simply that both in Stalin's and Khrushchev's time the depth of their belief in the system and in their future was still quite pronounced. This optimistic attitude appears deeply shaken. What remains now are great-power ambitions, an ideologically oriented outlook on the world that breeds inertia, private careerism and materialism, and spiritual emptiness. In the difficult 1980s, a period of scarcities and austerity, it will be much harder to achieve a peaceful consensus among leadership groups and bureaucracies.

A typical political fissure in the 1980s is growing out of the competition of four Soviet areas—European Russia, the Ukraine, Siberia, and Central Asia—for scarce growth resources. European Russia and the Ukraine have developed industrial infrastructures but lack natural resources and labor. Siberia is rich in natural resources but lacks any industrial infrastructure and labor. Central Asia has major new sources of labor but lacks both an industrial infrastructure and natural resources. The competition for resources among representatives of each of those areas and the leaders in Moscow could usher in a period of intense struggle and rivalry.

A final political challenge that will confront the Soviet leadership in the 1980s is that of economic reform. The Soviet political and economic system can be described as institutionalized crisis- and emergency-management. Anyone watching a Soviet factory operating in a December when the last chance to fulfill the annual plan still exists, or a harvest that requires the mobilization, so it seems, of every white-collar worker, every student, and even every military unit in the district, knows that this is true. There is even a special, untranslatable word in the Soviet dictionary to describe this movement from one emergency to another. In the past, emergencies could be dealt with by the old and tried methods of mobilizing massive quantities of labor, resources, capital and land. These methods are no longer possible or productive. What is presently needed is *intensive* growth, and the political and economic systems are not constructed to deal with it. The question is no longer whether Soviet leaders will engage in significant reforms or will simply "muddle through," but rather whether they will improve the system or will "muddle down."

The chances of radical reform are very slight. "Minireforms," on the other hand, such as incentives for managers and workers to improve the quality of production or lower production costs, can change individual *aspects* of the Soviet planning system, but eventually they are absorbed by the system. Radical reforms, such as replacing administrative orders from Moscow on what and how to produce with decisionmaking at the factory, mine or construction organization level, would change the planning system itself and lead in the direction of market socialism. But this type of reform was never seriously tried by the Soviet leadership. The Soviet political leadership, after all, is similar to political elites in other countries: they prefer continuity to changes which might weaken their power.

Only when economic survival appears in question, of which there is no sign as yet, may the political rewards of abstaining from radical reform become less attractive than the political price to be paid for a reform. It may be that only a dramatic "revolution from above," forced upon the society by an unchallengeable leader like Stalin, would succeed in promoting such change. Not only is this type of leader not on the horizon and probably not possible in Russia in the foreseeable future, but his reforms would probably go in the opposite direction from those discussed here, which call for the devolution of political powers.

Today, when the number of absolutely top priorities has increased dramatically, the ability to accomplish them requires not simply a mobilization and concentration of resources but the balanced growth of the economy as a whole. The Polish economist Oskar Lange noted that the essence of the Soviet economy can best be described as a war economy in peacetime. Such a war economy no longer seems effective.

There are indications that the lack of balanced development

and the shallowness of technological development are starting to affect the military sector of the economy, primarily the quality of input and output. Draftees into the Soviet armed forces are ill-prepared from the point of view of education and skills to serve in a technologically modern army. The barrier between the civilian and military economic sectors which prevents a feedback from the military to the civilian sectors impedes the qualitative progress of the military sector. There is little doubt about the Soviet ability to "keep up with the Joneses" in the quality of their military buildup, but without a change in the *entire* Soviet economy, this process will be more difficult and more costly than in the past.

3

The Andropov
Succession

When Brezhnev departed the scene, for honorable burial in the Kremlin wall, he left his successors a crowded agenda. Most successions call for a reassessment, but the present transition in Moscow demands special attention because it coincides with major changes in the domestic and international environment that influence the formulation of policy and constitute a severe test of the Soviet political system, its balance and stability.

When Andropov became general secretary of the party, the most dramatic and crucial phase of the Soviet leadership succession started. In contrast to the past, the struggle for the leader's mantle began well before his death and intensified after the death of the chief Soviet ideologue, Mikhail A. Suslov, in the beginning of 1982. With the debilitating illness of the organizational secretary of the party, Andrei P. Kirilenko, by tradition the heir apparent, Politburo member Konstantin U. Chernenko became the key contender for the top position. Chernenko took over many of the duties of Kirilenko and, with the progressive decline of Brezhnev's health, became the man in charge of the day-to-day running of the top party institutions. A protégé of Brezhnev with a very undistinguished record and career, he was evidently Brezhnev's choice for the top position. The May 1982 transfer of Andropov from the chairmanship of the KGB to the party secretariat, by majority decision of the Politburo (it could only have been a decision of the Politburo to effect such a transfer), provided evidence of the sharp decline of Brezhnev's power and underscored divisions within the Politburo.

If Brezhnev had retired at the time of Andropov's transfer—and his transformation from a power behind the throne to a contender for the throne—it is our belief that Chernenko would have succeeded Brezhnev. Brezhnev's death in office, on the other hand, favored the candidacy of Andropov. With Brezhnev gone, Chernenko could no longer count on the commitment of Brezhnev's loyalists. Andropov's key card was his reputation as a strong leader and a generalist, a combination in short supply within the present Politburo. The coalitions which supported him probably included some of the oldest members of the Politburo and some of the youngest members of the Secretariat. The old generation (including probably civilian Minister of Defense Dmitri F. Ustinov, who due to his age was not a contender) felt more comfortable with a contemporary who had a distinguished career of his own than with Chernenko, whose entire career was that of companion to Brezhnev. The young secretaries of the Central Committee probably wanted a change and a strong leader from among the younger members of the old generation. Andropov fitted their credentials.

Profile of a Leader

The personality, the vision and style of the leader make a major difference in Soviet politics and policies. What do we know about Andropov that would help us anticipate his type of leadership? He is a Russian, born in 1914, the son of a middle-class railroad employee—the first Soviet top leader from the time of Lenin who is not of worker or peasant origin. He belongs to the Brezhnev generation of political activists for whom Stalin's great purge opened possibilities of quick advancement. From the age of 32 to 37 he was a professional functionary of the Young Communist League and then of the party apparatus. From 1951 till 1967 he worked in the East European affairs department of the party's Central Committee, where, after a four-year stint as ambassador to Hungary (he was there at the time of the 1956 Hungarian revolution), he rose to the position of the secretary of the Central Committee responsible for the Soviet external empire. In 1967 he was appointed by Brezhnev to the all-important post of the chief of the Soviet secret police and intelligence service, the KGB, a position which he held longer than any of his predecessors.

His formal education was very spotty. Aside from graduating from a vocational school of inland-water transportation, he attended a provincial university, where he studied Marxist-Leninist philosophy, and the highest Communist party school in Moscow, but he did not finish either. Yet by all accounts he is a sophisticated individual whose knowledge and tastes have been acquired through self-education.

Although he has never set foot in a non-Communist country, his preparation to guide Soviet foreign policy is impressive. His experience in managing the troubled and troublesome Soviet East European empire is second to none. His knowledge of internal Soviet policies and politics, including the politics of the non-Russian areas, is extensive. With his KGB background he is the leader most qualified to enforce law, order and discipline in Soviet society. Where he lacks experience is in the management of the Soviet economy. In this respect, he will have to rely heavily on the present directors or bring in his own economic specialists.

By all accounts Andropov is a complex individual, a strong leader with an extraordinary political sense and subtlety—a major departure from the shrewd but simple leaders who preceded him in the post-Stalin era. He is simultaneously respected and feared by Soviet party and government leaders. This much we know about Andropov. We also know that his actual and potential authority is enormous. He monopolizes key posts of command—general secretary of the party, chairman of the Politburo, and, as chairman of the Supreme Soviet, the head of state. His key power resource is the support of the KGB and of a part of the professional party apparatus, the single largest bloc in top decisionmaking, executive and largely honorific bodies.

WHERE THE POWER LIES

The Communist party of the Soviet Union holds all political power, centered in the Politburo and the Secretariat of the Central Committee. All the important decisions—in foreign policy, the

THE PARTY

Communist Party Congress
Theoretically the highest body. Consists of delegates elected by party organizations around the country and meets once in five years (it last met in 1981). The congress elects:

The Central Committee
Consists of several hundred members picked from among congress delegates. Acts for the congress between sessions and meets about twice a year to discuss and approve policies. It elects what are, in effect, the two highest party bodies:

The Politburo
Sets the overall policy of the country. Consists of about a dozen full (voting) members and about eight or nine candidate (nonvoting) members, all of whom are among the leading political figures of the Soviet Union. Membership is not a position in itself; all members serve ex officio and have regular fulltime duties in either the party or the government.

FULL MEMBERS: Geidar Aliyev, Yuri V. Andropov, Konstantin U. Chernenko, Mikhail S. Gorbachev, Viktor V. Grishin, Andrei A. Gromyko, Dinmukhamed A. Kunayev, Grigory V. Romanov, Vladimir V. Shcherbitsky, Nikolai A. Tikhonov, Dmitri F. Ustinov.

The Secretariat
Actually runs the day-to-day affairs of the Soviet Union. Headed by the general secretary, who was Mr. Brezhnev, and assisted by a number of secretaries and a large permanent staff.

MEMBERS: Mr. Andropov, Mr. Chernenko, Vladimir I. Dolgikh, Mr. Gorbachev, Ivan V. Kapitonov, Boris N. Ponomarev, Konstantin V. Rusakov, Nicolai I. Ryzhkov, Mr. Romanov, Mikhail V. Zimyanin.

IN THE SOVIET UNION

economy, and social affairs—are made there and carried out by the subordinate apparatus of the government and by the nominal legislature, which lacks independent power.

THE GOVERNMENT

Supreme Soviet of the U.S.S.R.
Counterpart of the party congress and the nominal parliament, which is "elected" every five years from a single slate of candidates handpicked by the leadership. Meets perfunctorily twice a year to approve legislation drafted by the leadership and selects two key government bodies:

Council of Ministers
The actual government, which is headed by the Prime Minister (now Mr. Tikhonov) and consists of a First Deputy Prime Minister and a number of Deputy Prime Ministers as well as the various Ministers and agency chairmen. The Prime Minister and his Deputy Prime Ministers make up a kind of inner circle in the government known as the Presidium of the Council of Ministers.

Presidium of the Supreme Soviet
Performs functions of the nation's president and is headed by a chairman, the actual President (Mr. Andropov), and a number of deputy chairmen (in effect Vice Presidents). The First Vice President is Vasily V. Kuznetsov.

NOTE: The Soviet leadership group is, in effect, made up of all the members of the Politburo and all the members of the Secretariat. They constitute the inner circle of the Soviet hierarchy and make all major decisions. Those who are in both the fulltime Secretariat and the Politburo (ex officio) are probably the key people in the Soviet Union.

When Andropov was elevated to general secretary of the party, it was the first time in Soviet history that an individual who had been out of the party apparatus for 15 years assumed this position. While Andropov was not *in* the party apparatus for a long time, he is clearly *of* the party apparatus. Of the 47 years of Andropov's active political life, he spent 27 years as a functionary of the party.

As chairman of the powerful Defense Council, Andropov oversees the Soviet military-industrial complex. He also supervises the *nomenklatura,* that is, the system of appointments and dismissals of holders of key offices throughout all the bureaucracies.

After a year in office, Andropov's actual power far surpasses that of his two predecessors at a comparable stage. This is so because Soviet bureaucratic leadership groups feel a need for a strong chief and regard Andropov as such; there are no obvious competitors among the top leadership after what appears to be Chernenko's irreversible defeat (he was replaced in October 1983 as head of the party's General Department); and Andropov's style of leadership, with its preference for gradualism in personnel and policy changes, has not provoked the formation of opposition coalitions or the sabotage of policies within the bureaucracies.

New Broom

The most noticeable contrasts between Brezhnev's last autumn and Andropov's first spring were the disappearance of the black marketeer from the select rooms of the Aragvy restaurant and the hesitation of the taxi driver to insist on payment in hard currency. The general mood in Moscow, however, is harder to define. The ordinary Muscovite, it seems, is slipping back into his normal state of political apathy after an initial burst of expectations that followed Andropov's accession. His wish that Andropov prove a new *khoziain,* a boss who would get things moving again, is yielding to suspicion that nothing much seems to be happening apart from a few changes in detail.

This popular attitude is not shared by many members of the Soviet political elite, experts in academic institutions, and a segment of the in-system intelligentsia. For them the slow start indicates not a want of ideas and capacities but rather a gradualist approach and a methodical preparation characteristic of Andropov's style of work, one that augurs a genuine and durable farewell to Brezhnev's paralysis. Their sentiments are reflected in a story circulating among them. When appointed chairman of the KGB in 1967, Andropov reportedly assembled all top personnel from around the country and delivered a speech. "I don't know much about your work," he said. "I'm not a professional. I want you to feel secure in helping me learn what you do and in giving me advice." One year later, very few in his audience remained at their old jobs; they had been fired, promoted, or transferred. Two years later, the story concludes, Andropov's control of the KGB apparatus and operations was indisputable, and his innovative policies had begun to affect the activities and operating methods of this immensely powerful institution. Those who recounted the story clearly hoped that Andropov would follow a similar course in his new and vastly more significant position. There is a high probability that their hopes will be realized, if only Andropov's health sustains him.

The average Muscovite and the Western observer can see very little of Andropov's planning and long-range goals. Most striking has been the now-flagging campaign Andropov launched shortly after assuming office calling for greater candor in relations between leadership and population. The Soviet press openly reports that serious shortages of food and consumer goods exist, that bureaucratic foot-dragging is pervasive, that economic plans remain notoriously unfulfilled, that a major share of allocated investments is frozen, and that wages and income will not rise without a significant improvement in labor productivity.

There has been a campaign to convince the public that there is movement and that the new leader is hard at work, on top of his job, and capable of resolving the difficulties inherited from Brezhnev. Unprecedented are the press announcements of weekly Politburo meetings, containing information on the agenda and the results of the deliberations.

Most important and impressive, this campaign has also been

aimed at enforcing greater discipline in the workplace and society-at-large as well as reducing blatant official and unofficial corruption. The immediate effects of these efforts are evident even to outsiders: worker absenteeism has declined; bureaucrats display a greater sense of responsibility; and a goodly number of illegal private traders no longer stake out the environs of tourist hotels. In all probability it is the stress on social discipline among workers and greater responsibility among managers and bureaucrats that accounted in large part for the overfulfillment of the Soviet industrial production plan in the first quarter of 1983.

These cosmetic changes will have little lasting effect, however, on the performance of the economy and the conduct of the citizenry. Much more important are the deeper, less-visible currents of activity that suggest preparations for change. These currents affect personnel, institutional functions, and ideological orientation.

Personnel changes have only begun at upper-middle and top levels of the party-state machine. In the Politburo, Kirilenko was retired and the former chief of the Azerbaijan KGB and later first secretary of the Azerbaijan party, Geidar A. Aliyev, was elected to full membership and appointed first deputy prime minister. Politburo member and Minister of Foreign Affairs Andrei A. Gromyko has become a first deputy prime minister. On a lower but still important level of the party-state bureaucracy, a few dozen officials have been fired (some were arrested), transferred, or promoted in ways reflecting their competence and loyalty to Andropov.

Another phase of Andropov's emerging program is the redefinition of functions in key party and state institutions. Potentially significant is the newly defined jurisdiction of the new party secretary for economic affairs, Nikolai Ryzhkov. He is empowered to transform the function of the central party's economic apparatus from detailed supervision of the state economic bureaucracies to a primary concern with strategic planning and the formulation of economic reforms.

Appointments within the state bureaucracy similarly suggest greater centralization and greater control of the state bureaucracy from within. Two additional first deputy prime ministers, both members of the Politburo, were named and have been given newly created jurisdictions. The first, Andropov's friend Aliyev, known for his determined fight against corruption in Azerbaijan, can be expected to apply this experience to the all-union government. A veritable "new broom," he has been named to control and supervise the state bureaucracy. The second, Foreign Minister Gromyko, will now supervise and coordinate virtually all government activities relating to foreign affairs (excluding, presumably, the intelligence activities). His responsibilities include the making of foreign policy, technology transfers, participation in international financial arrangements, and Soviet export industries. These two appointments erode dramatically the jurisdiction of the ailing Prime Minister Nikolai A. Tikhonov.

Reorganization may also affect the little-known Defense Council, the top decisionmaking body in military, military-political, and military-economic matters. Chaired by Andropov, as it was by his predecessor, the council includes, in addition to the minister of defense and his principal military commanders, the prime minister and key civilian managers of military industries, the head of the KGB, and the minister of foreign affairs. Without a sizable staff of its own, the tasks of setting the agenda of meetings, preparing briefings, and presenting options fall to military experts of the General Staff who thereby exert considerable influence. It is said that Andropov plans to establish an independent staff for the Defense Council, one composed in part of civilian, in part of military, specialists permanently transferred to the council from the Ministry of Defense and General Staff. This severing of the connection between the staffs of the Ministry of Defense and General Staff could offer Andropov greater flexibility in dealing with proposals and requests emanating from the armed forces.

Another Andropov initiative is the preparation of ideological arguments and justifications for organizational, administrative and economic changes. Novel ideological formulas that have begun to appear in speeches and articles by Andropov and some associates will soon be broadcast by an army of professional propaganda experts to prepare the enormous party and state bureaucracies and the population-at-large for reforms to come. The two most important of the new formulas concern "the potential of growth in socialist society" and "contradictions in the development of mature socialist societies."

According to the first formula, the alleged superiority of socialist over capitalist societies is now said to constitute only a "potential" which will not be realized unless wisely exploited by the directors of socialist society and vigorously pursued by the workers. The clear implication, at times explicitly stated, is that at present and in the immediate past this potential has not been properly nurtured.

According to the second formula, contradictions occur constantly between the potential of Soviet development and the actual growth and development of the means of production, particularly new technology. To overcome such contradictions and to take full advantage of the unrealized potential inherent in the socialist organization of labor, Soviet economic mechanisms and organizations must be continuously adjusted and reformed. Both formulas, firmly planted in the garden of quotations from the "holy writ," alert bureaucrats, managers, and the populace to the necessity of reforms which are to be regarded as products of the "law of socialist development."

Changes in personnel, institutional functions, and ideological formulations all point to an accumulation of greater power by a leader bent on preparing the ground for change. The important question is how Andropov will use his power. The impulsive Khrushchev used his power in a formidable effort to restructure the Stalinist system of rule. Less ambitious was the cautious and circumspect Brezhnev who used his power to reverse many of Khrushchev's reforms (the so-called harebrained schemes).

Andropov, unlike Khrushchev, will probably design and execute reforms only after thorough preparation, and he will secure broad support within the leadership. Unlike Brezhnev he will probably push reforms beyond the limits of consensus to challenge vested interests of high-level bureaucrats. If Khrushchev pursued reform mainly through structural change and Brezhnev pursued

Photo by Marcel Minnée

The potatoes these women are selling were grown on one of many private farm plots, a source of food for the Soviet consumer.

it mainly through policies of budgetary allocation, Andropov, in the author's opinion, will most likely combine both approaches. His main domestic objectives will be the inculcation of strong social discipline in white- and blue-collar workplaces and the introduction of innovations into management of the economy.

Agriculture must be given top priority because of the critical role it plays in the economy and society. For Soviet citizens, food is the single most important and largest item in their budgets. For the government, its availability is a decisive guarantor of social stability and the significant foundation on which rests the effectiveness of incentives essential for higher industrial productivity.

It seems almost certain that the new form of "contract brigade," successfully tested in the southern Soviet Union, especially Georgia, will be extended throughout the largest republic of all—the Russian Republic. The contract brigade bands together two dozen farmers, tractor drivers and mechanics who sign a contract with their collective farm that fixes the size of the crop they will produce on a specific piece of collective farmland and the remuneration each will receive. Members of the brigade retain any surplus, thus assuring strong interest in personal and group labor.

Andropov will probably also relax rules affecting the collective farmer's private plot, the impressive source of vegetables, fruits, dairy products and meat for Soviet consumers. Current discussions mention the abolition of limits on the number of livestock owned by individual farmers; permission for grazing private cattle on collective land; provision of credits, fertilizers and implements from the collective farm to individual farmers. In addition, industrial enterprises are being encouraged to provision their own workers by investing where possible in farms and truck gardens.

Andropov is also trying to improve coordination among all central and provincial agricultural institutions. These measures will succeed only if he can overcome countless bottlenecks resulting from the appalling underdevelopment of agriculture's infrastructure. That will be extremely expensive, but it will bring improvements in production in the first two or three years of Andropov's leadership. These can only be deemed minireforms, however, when contrasted to the People's Republic of China, which has introduced economic incentives and is returning decisionmaking in agriculture to the household level, or to Hungary, which has transformed collective farms into quasi-capitalist enterprises.

No authoritative statement has yet heralded any far-reaching reforms in Soviet industry, desirable as they would be. The leadership's reluctance derives, in part at least, from the great degree to which industrial reforms impinge on deeply vested interests of ministerial, planning and managerial bureaucracies, the intermediate levels of the party apparatus, and even the industrial workers who would have to work harder with little immediate reward.

A program of marginal reforms, which will include measures

of both centralization and decentralization, will probably be presented in the near future to the plenum of the Central Committee.

As budgetary decisions are made, one critical dilemma faces the new leadership—the level and distribution of funds for military growth. Andropov's dilemma is not only guns versus butter, as so often presented in the West. It is the choice between maintaining current direct expenditures on arms and upkeep of military forces versus large-scale investment in the military-industrial plant to support future military growth. As long as Soviet industrial output was growing annually by 4 to 5 percent, direct Soviet military expenditures could also grow annually by about 5 percent, while at the same time the level of investment in the military-industrial plant remained very high. If the current annual growth rate of about 2.5 percent persists throughout the decade, direct military expenditures cannot continue to grow at the 1970s level without depressing the growth rate of military-industrial development. To maintain both at 1970s levels is not possible.

It seems that some military leaders advocate steady growth of direct military expenditures over military-industrial plant investment, while some civilian leaders advocate cuts in direct military growth to permit greater military-industrial investment. With the expected decline in overall economic performance, this conflict will become sharper and reconciliation of the two kinds of expenditures more difficult. Whether, as some anticipate, Andropov decides to preserve investment growth, at the expense of reducing the growth of direct military expenditures, will depend on the level of Western military spending and his evaluation of the East-West military balance. There will not be, in any case, a return to high growth rates in both areas, even in the 1990s, without a major economic reform. Such a reform will be less likely and more costly if Andropov continues to consume potential growth resources for military purposes.

Conversations with Soviet officials confirm that there are no plans for radical decentralizing reforms. Nevertheless, economic performance can and will be improved somewhat, in the author's

Barling in *The Christian Science Monitor* © 1983 TCSPS

opinion, at least in the first years. There is so much slack and irrationality in the economic system that determined leadership can mobilize this unused potential to considerable effect. From speeches by Andropov and his associates and from discussions in professional journals, it appears that the reform program that is emerging will include the following elements: a national planning system that is modernized and computerized; unified and centralized national energy networks; increased labor mobility from low- to high-resource areas; and a major shake-up and personnel replacement in management and planning institutions.

Such minireforms, at least initially, may accomplish marginal improvements. Yet to all who remember the history of industrial reform in the post-Stalin period, such piecemeal measures will not radically alter the inefficient economic system and will eventually be absorbed and neutralized by that system.

Why Radical Reforms Are Unlikely

There are many reasons why radical economic change in the Soviet Union is unlikely, even under strong leadership. The vested interests opposing such change are very powerful and will remain so even when there is a high turnover in the bureaucracies and leadership and when the pressure to get the country moving again intensifies. As one author has aptly remarked: "After 60 years of experience with a socialist economy run by government agencies . . . nearly everyone seems to have found ways to turn its shortcomings to individual advantage."

The initiative for reform in the face of widespread opposition has to come from a *strong leadership,* especially from the general secretary. Even assuming that Andropov becomes convinced of the necessity for far-reaching reforms—and this is a very big assumption—it will take a long time until he is strong enough to make serious efforts in this direction. If our predictions are correct, Andropov is only an interim leader who will not have enough time to infuse the *nominal* position of first secretary with the *real* powers required to push for radical reform. Such a leader may emerge only during the second succession, but, if the past is any indication, it will take him many years to amass the necessary powers.

As noted above, under Brezhnev the leadership became increasingly dependent on the expertise and advice of professional groups. Stephen F. Cohen, professor of politics at Princeton University, is probably quite right when he stresses that the spirit of reform and liberalism is not dead in the U.S.S.R.—only dormant. It is among the professional groups, especially among the economists, that one would probably find the greatest support for radical reforms. However, these groups are fragmented and divided over what kinds of reforms are needed. They are also easily manipulated by the various factions in the leadership. If they continue to speak with a divided voice, they will neutralize their potential for influencing liberal reform.

One should not minimize the purely economic and technical difficulties of a thorough reform in the Soviet Union. It would most certainly involve a temporary decline in production and in productivity, would significantly increase the need for real incentives, and would entail the enormous task of reeducating the labor force and management. The difficult transitional period would require very large reserves of capital and consumer goods. In the 1980s, a period when the Soviet economy will be stretched to its outer limits, radical reform will be extremely difficult. The political risks of attempting a thorough reform during a period of economic decline must seem very great to the leadership, probably graver than the consequences of living with the old system.

When considering a thorough—or even timid—liberalizing reform in the Soviet Union, Soviet leaders must weigh its potential impact upon Eastern Europe. Eastern Europe is often regarded as the funnel through which Western influence and reformist tendencies are channeled to the Soviet Union. There is some truth to this assertion, but more often Eastern Europe is a thoroughly conservative influence on the *domestic* Soviet scene. By its very existence, the Soviet East European empire increases the political price—and political dangers—of far-reaching economic reform in the Soviet Union. Liberal forces in Eastern Europe could interpret a reform program as a signal that the Soviet leadership would tolerate economic and maybe even political liberalization. Because it would encourage the forces of liberalism in Eastern Europe, domestic reform would endanger Soviet rule over its East European empire. In these circumstances, it would require an enormously confident—or desperate—Soviet leadership to initiate such policies. The situation in Eastern Europe in the 1980s will probably be very difficult economically, explosive socially, and precarious politically, and will influence the Soviet leadership not to undertake reforms.

The multination and nominally federal Soviet system also exerts a conservative influence on reformers. During the Brezhnev period, relations between the centrally dominant Russians and the non-Russians were relatively peaceful, but the balance of those relations is quite precarious. To institute a thorough liberalizing economic reform in the Soviet Union could—and probably would—upset that balance. It would entail a major delegation of power to the bureaucrats on the provincial and local level. One can imagine the Soviet leaders considering such a transfer of power in Russia proper, but scarcely to the non-Russian republics, where it would concentrate major power in the hands of ethnically non-Russian officials. This would inevitably reinforce their ambitions for autonomy and could strengthen dangerous separatist tendencies.

A thorough liberalizing reform would also require a basic change in the working style of the leadership, bureaucrats and professionals. The old leaders believe in the basic viability of the present system, although they recognize many of the shortcomings. The new younger leaders are much less patient with the system's deficiencies; some of them may even be fed up with it. But the basic impression one gets is that they do not feel that the system's potentials are exhausted. Instead they believe it is not well run and that they could run it much better—an attitude that is typical of successors in all countries.

A key obstacle to successful reform involves the way it is implemented. To be effective, far-reaching reforms must be carried out across-the-board without hesitation and not in piecemeal fashion. But until the results of a reform are tested and prove effective, the necessary determination and persistence will most likely be lacking.

Some might consider this analysis unduly pessimistic. It is always easier, of course, to predict continuities on the basis of past experience. The difficulty in foreseeing discontinuities lies exactly in the fact that past patterns of behavior and past experiences can give little guidance to the analyst. Yet, in this author's view, the past pattern of hesitant and ineffectual reform will continue to persist in the period of Andropov's leadership.

4

Soviet Foreign Policy
Under Andropov

The Soviet Union remains in an ascendant phase of great-power ambitions to which the messianic traditions of Russian nationalism and revolutionary Marxism-Leninism add momentum. The achievement of strategic parity with the United States, the ability to project Soviet and proxy military forces far from Soviet borders, and the unceasing determination to guarantee Soviet participation in the regulation and resolution of every major international issue and regional conflict—all are signs that proclaim Soviet commitment to an active and expansionist global policy.

While the general tendency of Soviet foreign policy makes it dynamic, assertive and ambitious in the long run, its tactics in the short run oscillate between expansionism and retrenchment. At present Soviet foreign policy can best be described as a holding operation. Characterized by great caution, it neither displays major initiatives nor attempts to shape a new general line following the collapse of détente with the United States.

One reason for the sluggishness of current Soviet foreign policy is the dilemma over the behavior of the United States. If it appears to the Soviet leaders that President Ronald Reagan will be replaced in 1984 and that the pendulum in American politics, as many times in the past, will swing to the left, they will tend to keep Soviet foreign policy in a holding pattern. To the extent that Russian leaders take Reagan's anti-Soviet rhetoric and policy gestures seriously, they may be unwilling to test the Administration's resolve—thus also reinforcing existing policy.

To stress this particular explanation for current Soviet retrenchment strengthens the arguments of those Reagan advisers who insist on the correctness of the present U.S. foreign policy course. It would be wrong to draw such conclusions, however. These and other factors fail to challenge seriously the general proposition that the present phase of Soviet policy is a transitory phenomenon.

Another important reason for the cautiousness of current Soviet policy today is Soviet fear of overextension. The seemingly endless war in Afghanistan, the continuing investment in leftist governments in Africa, the burden of subsidies to Eastern Europe and Cuba, and especially the situation in Poland, all of these considerations dictate retrenchment rather than extension of commitment. In Poland, the policies of martial law and the crackdown on the trade union movement Solidarity, for which the Soviets pressed, spared them the incalculably great cost of an invasion, and paid off in the short run. The immediate benefits notwithstanding, the situation in Poland is stalemated. The embarrassing replacement of the Communist party by a military regime, far from being a temporary "solution," persists. Passive defiance of the Polish population continues unabated. And the catastrophic economic situation, according to official Polish estimates, will endure for a number of years before pre-Solidarity levels can be regained. Most important, Polish Communists and Soviet leaders have proved helpless in devising a realistic plan to restore political and economic stability.

The crisis situation in Poland that will persist for a long time has a number of military consequences: it is doubtful that Polish elite units can be included in Soviet war plans vis-à-vis NATO because they will be needed at home to assure the docility of the Polish population; it puts in question the loyalty of Polish troops,

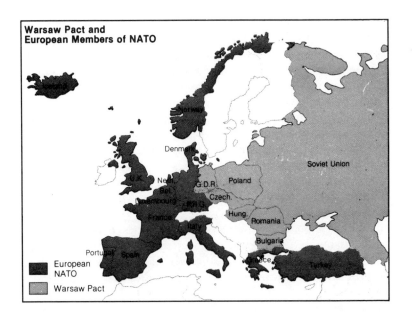

who are drafted, to Soviet goals; it raises the problem of the
security of the Polish supply and communication "corridor" to
Soviet front-line troops in East Germany, and forces the Soviets,
in their contingency plans in the event of a war with NATO, to
develop alternative routes of supply and communication through
the southern route to Czechoslovakia; it requires, in case of war
with NATO, the deployment of major Soviet forces in a hostile
Poland to assure the security of the Soviet rear. All in all, the
Polish situation bears a stamp of provisionality where one false
move can still provoke an explosion.

Another reason for not making any major changes in Soviet
foreign policy for the time being has to do with Soviet-West
European relations. While détente with the United States has
unraveled, détente with Western Europe continues to prosper as
it did in the early 1970s. Commercial relations flourish. Points of
conflict like Berlin remain dormant. A West European commit-

ment to increased military expenditures has been postponed. Both inside and especially outside government circles, there has been an immense growth in West European opposition to the agreed deployment of U.S. intermediate-range nuclear weapons in Europe, an issue of central importance to the Soviet Union.

Soviet policymakers hope that the mutually beneficial and benign Soviet-West European relations will induce West European governments to become intermediaries in Soviet-American relations, to act as a pressure group in tempering the extremes of American policy toward the Soviets, to serve as a catalyst in propelling the United States toward a resumption of serious dialogue. Even if actual events fall short of this goal, the Soviets hope at least to achieve a further widening of the split in the NATO alliance. Given the present state of East-West relations, with its partial détente and a bellicose United States, the Soviet script calls for a peace offensive, a posture of injured innocence, and an image of good sense and reasonableness displayed to the outside world. (Of course, the downing of the Korean Air Lines civilian jet in September 1983 and the way in which the Soviet leaders dealt with this incident did much to undermine the Soviet peace offensive.)

The relatively quiescent Soviet foreign policy today is also a reflection of a period of political transition, which was apparent publicly even before Brezhnev died. During a succession period the two key goals of the Soviet leadership are to insulate domestic politics and policies from foreign crises and challenges, and to preserve, stabilize and protect Soviet allies and client-states from foreign incursions. The Andropov leadership is likely to display considerable caution in its expansionist drive, at least initially. At the same time it is likely to combine greater pliability in arms-control negotiations with concerted efforts to fan the growth of peace movements in the West and to launch a major peace offensive in Western Europe and the United States.

The holding pattern in Soviet foreign policy, it should be repeated, in no way affects the basic directions of Soviet interest. The Soviets are determined that both the overall and regional military balance remain unchanged. They continue directly or through surrogates to send their clandestine matériel support to revolutionary or anti-status quo forces. They expect only gain from a low profile. They wait for the deepening of crisis in the Western alliance. They hope that small investments will enhance Soviet influence in revolutionary Iran. In short, at the present moment, for Soviet policymakers the tendency to profit from the troubles of others takes precedence over the tendency to make trouble for others.

Andropov has not yet undertaken a serious reorganization of the party-state foreign policy apparatus or major changes in its personnel. (As long as Gromyko retains major influence in determining foreign policy, any major change is probably unlikely.) Nor has he made key long-range and intermediate-range foreign policy decisions, including the course of relations to be pursued with the United States, which will probably be fixed only after the 1984 U.S. elections.

Andropov's short-term agenda consists of three main issues: installation of U.S. intermediate-range missiles in Western Europe, relations with China, and Eastern Europe.

The deployment of the U.S. intermediate-range nuclear forces (INF) in Europe was both the central issue for Soviet security and the first serious international test of Andropov's leadership. The first deployment of Pershing II and cruise missiles in West Germany took place, as scheduled, in November 1983. For both superpowers the political aspects of the INF decision superseded the military aspects. The United States regarded deployment as a symbol of its determination to alter the U.S.-Soviet military balance and to reassure West Europeans of its lasting commitment to the defense of Europe, and as a test of the cohesion of the Western alliance under Soviet pressure. The Soviet Union opposed deployment exactly because it was seen as a dangerous precedent, the beginning of a U.S. attempt to alter the nuclear balance of power. For the Soviets the fact of deployment is much more significant than the actual military importance of the missiles themselves. The main question for them is not the number of Pershing IIs and cruise missiles in Europe but *any* Pershing IIs and cruise missiles in Europe.

Because he felt he could not afford to lose his first test, Andropov did not make concessions great enough to prevent deployment. Instead he retaliated by announcing the deployment of seaborne nuclear missiles against the United States and abrogating the voluntary Soviet moratorium on deployment of SS-20s targeted on Western Europe. Only after both sides have deployed their weapons will serious negotiations begin—not simply regarding INF but the overall reduction and stabilization of strategic forces.

Andropov's second main short-term concern is China. Even before Brezhnev's death in November 1982, the virulence of the conflict between the two neighbors was abating and the slow movement toward normalization in state relations had begun. If in autumn 1982 Soviet specialists were stressing the slowness of the process and the unlikelihood it would alter the basic shape of the strategic Soviet-Chinese-American triangle, in the spring of 1983 they were arguing that the process would be quicker and broader than earlier anticipated. Some even spoke of improved relations at the party as well as state levels. The movement toward normalization, however, is taking place neither as fast as the Soviets would have us believe nor as slowly as the Chinese would have us believe.

The consequences of the normalization process for the United States should not be exaggerated. Normalization will bring no Sino-Soviet alliance, not even détente. It will only further strengthen China's position in the triangle, for China and the Soviet Union remain potential enemies who measure their security in terms of their adversary's weakness. With regard to the United States, the Chinese will continue to have little to fear and much to gain. The Chinese softening of preconditions for normalization with the Soviet Union stems less from specific American policies (although they are disturbed by U.S. relations with Taiwan and fearful of association with Reagan policies in the third world) than from China's need for good relations with its neighbors in order to pursue internal modernization. Reassured by Reagan's hard line against the Soviet Union, China can relax its warnings to us about Soviet hegemonism. Indeed, one can argue, it is an axiom that poor Soviet-American relations draw the Chinese toward the Soviet Union, while good Soviet-American relations draw them closer to the United States.

Andropov will no doubt pursue improved relations with China more successfully than his predecessor. Yet even a faster and broader normalization will not release the one quarter of Soviet armed forces presently stationed along the border with China. Nor will it facilitate the more central Soviet goals of destroying the Western alliance or restoring a semblance of détente with the United States. Some American politicians and experts appear disgruntled that we have "lost the China card," but the truth of the matter is we never had a China card to lose.

With regard to Eastern Europe, Andropov, like his three predecessors, is committed to domination. This empire represents for Soviet political leaders not only a major condition of security but the spoils of victory in World War II and, as such, a major source of legitimacy for the top leader, the bureaucrats and professionals, and the regime as a whole. The main danger is, of course, Poland. As the third year of military rule in Poland approaches, there are no firm plans either in Poland or the Soviet Union for rectifying the disastrous economic situation and restoring political stability. The danger of an explosion has been reduced by a crackdown on Solidarity's leadership, the imposition of martial law and the exhaustion of society. But the danger nevertheless remains, fanned by a restless population, a radicalized Church, and a sharply divided ruling group. The Soviet burden is all the heavier because of Poland's inability to meet contractual obligations to other Communist countries and the military consequences of Poland no longer being a dependable member of the Warsaw Pact. Andropov has apparently decided to minimize his economic losses by substantially reducing subsidies to Poland and preserving military rule, while closely monitoring the political situation.

Soviet worries in Eastern Europe do not end in Poland. It is clear to Soviet leaders that Eastern Europe has entered a prolonged period of economic difficulties, ranging from international credit stringencies to low growth rates and a stagnating

Photo by Marcel Minnée

**The memory of World War II and the defense of the homeland
in which millions of Soviet citizens lost their lives
is kept alive by exhibits such as the above.**

standard of living. These serious problems are equally evident in economically orthodox Czechoslovakia, managerially efficient East Germany, and reformist Hungary. Given the brittleness of governmental legitimacy in Eastern Europe, it is feared that economic failures will translate into social instability and political unrest.

The main lines of Andropov's policy toward Eastern Europe are taking shape. They call for much closer supervision of political orthodoxy, preemptive crackdowns on dissent, greater pressure against experimentation, and rapid reaction to social and political trouble. They include sharp reduction or even elimination of Soviet subsidies on oil and other raw materials to Eastern Europe so that Soviet trade will contribute more constructively to improving the troubled Soviet economy. They also include the more-energetic pursuit of an old and long-resisted goal of greater integration of the East European and Soviet economies with regard to division of labor, coordination of investments, technological exchange, and collective projects. Greater bloc interdependence, however, even if successful, may mask but it will not eliminate the inevitable threats to the social peace of the East European empire.

━━━━━━━━━━━━━━━━━━━━━━━━

Andropov has maintained a rather low profile in his first year. His accumulation of the power inherent in formal office is methodical and steady. His preparation for structural, organizational and economic innovations is gradual and slow. His conduct of foreign policy so far is cautious and flexible.

Yet by all accounts Andropov is a strong leader, concerned to leave his personal mark on the society he rules. He was 10 years older than either Khrushchev or Brezhnev when he assumed the office of general secretary, and much less healthy. He has little time to achieve what he wants for the Soviet Union and himself. One may expect that he will soon advance a clear and broad program of domestic adjustments and reforms which almost certainly will not change the system in any fundamental way but probably will counteract the sloth, inertia and rigidity of the late Brezhnev years. The systemic crisis which the Soviet Union faces is not one of survival but of effectiveness. If the effectiveness of the Soviet system is not improved during Andropov's tenure in office, future Soviet leaders may well face a crisis of survival.

5

Western Policies
Toward the Soviet Union

In the nuclear era there is no choice for either the United States or Western Europe but to negotiate with the Soviet Union on a broad range of issues and to strive for the dependable management of inevitable competition and conflict. The question is whether the Western alliance can influence the policies of the Soviet Union and, in particular, whether it can influence the choice of options open to the new Soviet leaders. My answer would be a qualified yes. Since any important action of the West clearly affects Soviet policy, the real question is whether our influence reflects deliberate effort as distinct from unintended consequence and whether such deliberate effort can be elaborated and sustained in the democratic environment of our own policy-making. In the last analysis our influence will depend in part on the choice of objectives with regard to Soviet policy and in part on our strength, unity, steadfastness and flexibility.

It is utterly utopian to believe that our influence on Soviet policies can lead to fundamental systemic change in the Soviet Union, a reorientation of Soviet policy from external to internal priorities, or an abandonment of any major arms buildup that Soviet leaders deem essential to the security of their country, their empire and their global stature. We cannot, moreover, significantly influence either the overall direction of Soviet foreign policy or the outcome of any alleged contest between Soviet "hawks" and "doves." What we can and should try to influence are the content of specific military and foreign policies, Soviet readiness to exploit foreign temptations, and the degree of moderation or extremism in overall Soviet international conduct. In the dangerous conditions of escalating nuclear armaments and world turmoil, even this modest influence may be a condition of survival.

The two central goals of Western policies toward the Soviet Union are to prevent Soviet expansion and to achieve an equitable balance of military power. It is misleading, therefore, to focus our attention, as is often done when discussing East-West relations, on narrowly formulated questions: Can Soviet-American détente be restored? Should the West European détente with the Soviet Union continue, given its potential for disrupting the Western alliance? The bundle of policies, ideas and expectations we call détente is neither good nor bad in itself. The real question is how effectively it serves our two main goals vis-à-vis the Soviet Union.

On this score, the détente of the 1970s did not pass the test of effectiveness, at least from the American point of view. Détente became in the United States a symbol of America's lack of will and of the failure of the Western alliance to preserve its unity and to influence constructively the international conduct of the Soviet Union. The word acquired a negative emotive meaning which went well beyond the actual suppositions and assumptions on which it rested. Let me therefore avoid this term and speak instead about the substance, forms and instruments of policies which have as their goals the management of East-West conflict and the restoration of East-West cooperation. Let us examine some of the lessons we have learned or should have learned from our experience in the 1970s and early 1980s.

The *internal* strength of the United States and West European countries is as important in formulating and implementing effective policies with regard to the Soviet Union as their *external* strength. Former Secretary of State Henry A. Kissinger's policy toward the Soviet Union during the early and mid-1970s was not wrong in itself. The expectations of what it could achieve, at what price, and how quickly were grossly exaggerated, however. That the policy collapsed was not the fault of either the policy or its chief architect but of the conditions that at the time prevailed in the United States and to some extent survive today—the post-Vietnam malaise, the depressed levels of military spending, the deleterious effects of Watergate on the American political system, particularly its executive branch.

The unity of the Western alliance is also essential in formulating policy toward the Soviet Union, especially in the choice of policy instruments used to influence Soviet international conduct. For the United States, the quest for unity is a frustrating experience. When the United States moves closer to the Soviet Union, its European allies fear a Soviet-American deal or Soviet-American condominium. When the United States moves away from the Soviet Union, its European allies fear that Europe will be dragged into confrontation with the Soviet Union or that the risk is heightened that war will be fought on European soil.

The pendulum of American policies toward the Soviet Union tends to swing from one extreme to another and leaves a disconcerting and accurate impression of unpredictability in both the Soviet Union and Western Europe. Indeed, the American political system and national character militate against the pursuit of a steady and steadfast policy toward the Soviet Union beyond, at best, the four-year tenure of a President. Potent forces work against a consistent policy—sensationalist media, a greatly weakened party system and tradition of bipartisanship in foreign policy, the tendency of the political public to view the Soviet Union in simplistic either/or terms rather than as an adversary with whom one both competes and cooperates.

The nature and range of instruments that were developed to influence Soviet foreign policies during the early and mid-1970s are quite broad. They include the escalation of the costs and risks of Soviet expansion, the manipulation of the Soviet fear of confrontation with the United States, the preservation of a just balance of military power, the offer of economic rewards and political and scientific cooperation, etc. No combination of those instruments and the policies they serve will solve miraculously our conflict with the Soviet Union, however. There are no quick fixes. The conflict can be regulated only through flexible and effective use of those instruments as disincentives and incentives. *Here a key lesson of the 1970s and early 1980s is that only when disincentives are credible, strong and continuous can incentives have any effect. But only when incentives are offered will disincentives have major effects.* The success of the skillful combination of incentives and disincentives will depend on reasoned agreement among the allies to coordinate their use and, in the last analysis, on the internal political, economic and military strength of the democracies.

The choices available to the West in composing its policy toward the Soviet Union are very often posed in terms of the very static and mutually exclusive options, namely détente, containment or confrontation. Taking into consideration the nature and goals of Soviet-Western relations, it is highly probable that containment, détente *and* confrontation will all characterize Soviet-Western, and particularly Soviet-American, relations in the 1980s. None of these approaches will dominate. Indeed, all three should be present as deliberate and coordinated policies of the Western alliance.

The need to manage and regulate East-West conflict and cooperation has increased dramatically with the escalating dangers of increasingly powerful and accurate nuclear weapons and an unceasing arms race. It is probably the first time in history—and the direct result of the nuclear revolution—that two contending alliance systems, separated by such deep divisions and sharp conflicts, have exhibited such a relatively high level of conflict management and cooperation. *In conditions of nuclear revolution, strategic parity, and mutual assured destruction, détente between West and East in one form or another is simply unavoidable.*

The scope, intensity and forms of détente between East and West may differ over time. But détente as a relatively stable and multifaceted relationship between East and West is necessary in the remaining decades of the 20th century if both the Soviet Union and the Western alliance wish to avoid a highly dangerous runaway arms race and the potentially destabilizing and unpredictable consequences of conflict, as well as to promote cooperation in areas where their interests overlap.

Avoidance of nuclear war, however, does not exhaust the needs and goals of the Western alliance. These include, for the Western alliance, and especially for the United States, the prevention of Soviet global expansion, the survival of independent and democratic systems in the West, and orderly and evolutionary change in third-world countries. A major dilemma for the Western alliance is how to arrest the multidirectional Soviet expansionism while at the same time minimizing the chances of nuclear escalation. If the policy of détente renders the competition more stable and thereby less dangerous, the policy of containing the Soviet Union is no less necessary and central. Indeed, *détente makes sense when it contains the expansion of Soviet power*. The policy of containment, its limitations, scope and central regional foci are of course subject to various interpretations within the Western alliance. The policy itself, however, implemented with determination and skill, is essential to our survival.

To contain Soviet power successfully can be done only by increasing substantially the costs and risks to the Soviets of the kind of international conduct we witnessed from 1975 to 1979. The Soviet Union, taking advantage of nuclear parity and the fear of nuclear escalation, will continue to exploit targets of opportunity in the third world. In the 1980s the Soviet Union will surely be strongly tempted to make use of direct and indirect military intervention in third-world turmoil—primarily in the Persian Gulf and Middle East—as it seeks to enhance its global-power position. The Western allies and particularly the United States have no choice but to make known their vital interests outside Europe and to prepare a credible response to Soviet expansion whenever those vital interests are threatened. For this response to be effective, the United States and Western Europe must be prepared for political, economic and military confrontation with the Soviet Union or its satellites. *The global—if selective—*

containment of Soviet power can be achieved only if the threat of East-West confrontation is credible.

Détente, containment and confrontation as policies of the Western alliance are not mutually exclusive. Their particular mix will depend as much on agreement within the alliance and on differing attitudes within Western countries, and particularly the United States, as it depends on Soviet international conduct.

In the 1980s, the key question is not what the new Soviet leader's foreign policies will be. It is rather what those of the Western alliance will be. What realistic goals should the Western allies pursue? Until the end of this century and probably even beyond, democratic nations have no choice but to face the conflict with the Soviet Union while at the same time striving to cooperate in the mutual interest of East and West. Let us hope that this conflict will retreat from the dangerous threshold of nuclear escalation and confrontation and that a united Western alliance can wait out the expansionist stage of Soviet development. Until this stage of Soviet national life passes, the United States and the Western alliance have no choice but to pursue a policy of containment, détente *and* confrontation toward the Soviet Union.

Talking It Over

A Note for Students and Discussion Groups

This issue of the HEADLINE SERIES, like its predecessors, is published for every serious reader, specialized or not, who takes an interest in the subject. Many of our readers will be in classrooms, seminars or community discussion groups. Particularly with them in mind, we present below some discussion questions—suggested as a starting point only—and references for further reading.

Discussion Questions

When Stalin died, the Soviet leadership issued a communiqué asking party members and the general public not to panic. When Brezhnev died, no appeal for calm was considered necessary. What are some of the major changes that have taken place on the Soviet political scene in the last 30 years?

How would you characterize the political legacies of Stalin, Khrushchev and Brezhnev? What was the principal characteristic of each one's rule?

Brezhnev left his successors a number of solid accomplishments, but he left an even greater number of difficult, unresolved problems. What were some of his domestic achievements? his achievements in the international arena? Do you agree with the author's definition of the Brezhnev era as "the era of external expansion of an internally declining power"?

What roles do dissent and repression play in the Soviet Union today? Has the role of dissent been exaggerated in the Western press?

The author writes that an irreversible process of decline has already started in the Soviet Union's "external empire" of Eastern Europe. What evidence does he cite to support his assertion?

In the 1980s the Soviet Union faces serious economic problems. What are the major obstacles to Soviet economic growth? What reforms would help overcome them? What is the likelihood that Andropov or his successor will undertake meaningful reforms?

If his health holds, what kind of leadership is Andropov likely to provide? How is his earlier career in the party, in Hungary and in the KGB likely to affect his leadership?

It is highly probable, in the author's view, that containment, détente *and* confrontation will characterize U.S.-Soviet relations in the 1980s. Are the three compatible? What is your view?

READING LIST

Bialer, Seweryn, *Stalin's Successors: Leadership, Stability and Change in the Soviet Union.* New York, Cambridge University Press, 1980. A careful study of changes in the Soviet political elite since Stalin's time.

Cohen, Stephen F., Rabinowitch, Alexander, and Sharlet, Robert, eds., *The Soviet Union Since Stalin.* Bloomington, Ind., Indiana University Press, 1980. A study of continuity and change in the Soviet Union, which traces the major trends and developments in politics, economics, sociology, culture and foreign policy.

Dmytryshyn, Basil, *USSR: A Concise History,* 3rd ed. New York, Scribner, 1978. The first half is a brief survey of Soviet history since 1917; the second half consists of a collection of hard-to-find documents.

Hoffmann, Erik P., and Fleron, Frederic J., eds., *The Conduct of Soviet Foreign Policy,* 2nd ed. New York, Aldine, 1980. An analysis of internal and external factors that shape Soviet policy and behavior.

Holzman, Franklyn D., "The Soviet Economy: Past, Present and Future." HEADLINE SERIES 260, September/October 1982. A concise introduction to the Soviet economy since Stalin's time, including a discussion of present difficulties.

Hough, Jerry F., and Fainsod, Merle, *How the Soviet Union Is Governed.* Cambridge, Mass., Harvard University Press, 1979. An updated version by Jerry Hough of Merle Fainsod's classic study.

McAuley, Mary, *Politics and the Soviet Union.* New York, Penguin, 1977. An assessment of the Soviet Union's political and economic framework.

Medvedev, Roy A., *Let History Judge: The Origins and Consequences of Stalinism.* A penetrating analysis of Stalinism.

Pankhurst, Jerry G., and Sacks, Michael Paul, eds., *Contemporary Soviet Society: Sociological Perspectives.* New York, Praeger, 1980. The monographs on life in the Soviet Union include a look at party politics, the link between educational level and power, various institutions, religions, rural society, and the status of women.

Smith, Hedrick, *The Russians.* New York, Quadrangle/New York Times Books, 1976. The former Moscow correspondent of *The New York Times* describes the Russian people, from the intellectual elites to the average working people and their daily lives.

Solzhenitsyn, Alexander I., *The Gulag Archipelago, 1918–1956,* 3 vols. New York, Harper and Row, 1974–1976. A memorial to millions of Soviet martyrs.

Tokes, Rudolf L., ed., *Dissent in the USSR: Politics, Ideology and People.* Baltimore, Md., Johns Hopkins University Press, 1975. A study of Soviet social roots and unorthodox behavior.

Ulam, Adam B., *Expansion and Coexistence: Soviet Foreign Policy, 1917–1973,* 2nd ed. New York, Praeger, 1973. A detailed account of the nature, trends and aims of Soviet foreign policy. The second edition includes the 1968 invasion of Czechoslovakia, the beginning of détente and the Middle East war of 1973.

Statement of Ownership, Management and Circulation

(Required by 39 U.S.C. 3685)

1a. Title of publication: Headline Series.

1b. Publication No: 00178780.

2. Date of filing: September 23, 1983.

3. Frequency of issue: Jan., March, May, Sept., Nov.

3a. No. of issues published annually: 5.

3b. Annual subscription price: $12.00.

4. Complete mailing address of known office of publication: 205 Lexington Ave., New York, N.Y. 10016.

5. Complete mailing address of the headquarters of general business offices of the publisher: Same.

6. Full names and complete mailing address of publisher, editor, and managing editor: Publisher—Foreign Policy Association, 205 Lexington Ave., New York, N.Y. 10016; Editor—Nancy Hoepli, FPA, 205 Lexington Ave., New York, N.Y. 10016.

7. Owner: (If owned by a corporation, its name and address must be stated and also immediately thereunder the names and addresses of stockholders owning or holding 1 percent or more of total amount of stock. If not owned by a corporation, the names and addresses of the individual owners must be given. If owned by a partnership or other unincorporated firm, its name and address, as well as that of each individual must be given. If the publication is published by a nonprofit organization, its name and address must be stated.) Foreign Policy Association, Inc., 205 Lexington Ave., New York, N.Y. 10016. No stockholders—a nonprofit corporation.

8. Known bondholders, mortgagees, and other security holders owning or holding 1 percent or more of total amount of bonds, mortgages or other securities (If there are none, so state) None.

9. For Completion by Nonprofit Organizations Authorized to Mail at Special Rates (Section 423.12 DMM only): The purpose, function, and nonprofit status of this organization and the exempt status for Federal income tax purposes (1) has not changed during preceding 12 months.

	10. Extent and Nature of Circulation	Average No. Copies Each Issue During Preceding 12 Months	Actual Number of Copies of Single Issue Published Nearest to Filing Date
A.	Total no. copies (net Press Run)	16,203	13,000
B.	Paid Circulation 1. Sales through dealers and carriers, street vendors and counter sales	5,756	1,406
	2. Mail subscription	7,463	7,242
C.	Total paid circulation (Sum of 10B1 and 10B2)	13,219	8,648
D.	Free distribution by mail, carrier or other means Samples, complimentary, and other free copies	800	430
E.	Total distribution (Sum of C and D)	14,019	9,078
F.	Copies not distributed 1. Office use, left over, unaccounted, spoiled after printing 2. Return from news agents	2,184 None	3,922 None
G.	Total (Sum of E, F1 and 2—should equal net press run shown in A)	16,203	13,000

11. I certify that the statements made by me above are correct and complete.

DON DENNIS
Vice President, Administration